PAKISTAN: "A BOAT UNDER TURBULENCE"

TABLE OF CONTENTS:

I. Introduction

    Background of Pakistan's Economy

II. The Economic Crisis

    A. Definition of the Crisis

    B. The Impact of the Crisis

    C. The Causes of the Crisis

III. The Historical Context

    A. The Early Years

    B. The Bhutto Era

    C. The Zia Years

    D. The Return of Democracy

IV. The Current Economic Landscape

    A. GDP and Growth

    B. Inflation and Interest Rates

    C. Fiscal Deficit and Public Debt

    D. Foreign Exchange Reserves and Exchange Rate

V. The Role of Agriculture

    A. Overview of Agriculture in Pakistan

    B. Issues with Agriculture

    C. Possible Solutions

VI. The Manufacturing Sector

    A. Overview of Manufacturing in Pakistan

    B. Issues with Manufacturing

C. Possible Solutions

VII. The Services Sector

A. Overview of Services in Pakistan

B. Issues with Services

C. Possible Solutions

VIII. Trade and Investment

A. Overview of Trade and Investment in Pakistan

B. Issues with Trade and Investment

C. Possible Solutions

IX. Infrastructure and Energy

A. Overview of Infrastructure and Energy in Pakistan

B. Issues with Infrastructure and Energy

C. Possible Solutions

X. Education and Health

A. Overview of Education and Health in Pakistan

B. Issues with Education and Health

C. Possible Solutions

XI. Governance and Corruption

A. Overview of Governance and Corruption in Pakistan

B. Issues with Governance and Corruption

C. Possible Solutions

XII. Conclusion

A. Summary of Findings

B. Recommendations

C. Final Thoughts

Book description:

Pakistan has experienced its fair share of economic upheaval over the years. From political instability to natural disasters, the country has encountered several hurdles that have hampered its economic growth. A multitude of reasons, including high inflation, insufficient foreign exchange reserves, and a significant fiscal deficit, have exacerbated Pakistan's present economic crisis.

This book will examine the reasons and consequences of Pakistan's current economic crisis. It will also look at the historical context of the crisis, including the numerous economic policies that have been pursued throughout the years. Furthermore, the book will look at Pakistan's current economic landscape, such as GDP and growth, inflation and interest rates, fiscal deficit and public debt, and foreign currency reserves and exchange rates.

The book will also look at the role of several economic sectors, such as agriculture, manufacturing, and services. It will investigate the difficulties confronting each of these industries as well as potential solutions. Furthermore, the book will look at trade and investment, infrastructure and energy, education and health, government and corruption, and the difficulties that each of these sectors is dealing with.

I. Introduction

Background of Pakistan's Economy

Pakistan's economy has a long and complicated history that has been impacted by a variety of internal and external causes. In 1947, the country earned independence from British colonial administration, and in the years thereafter, it has encountered various hurdles in developing a strong economy.

One of the most significant obstacles encountered by Pakistan was the subcontinent's partition, which resulted in the displacement of millions of people and the destruction of economic infrastructure. Agricultural production made for the majority of the country's GDP in the early years of independence.

The government gradually began to implement policies aimed at industrializing the country and diminishing its reliance on agriculture. As a result, the manufacturing sector expanded and became a primary driver of economic expansion throughout the 1960s and 1970s.

However, in the late 1970s and early 1980s, Pakistan experienced a number of external shocks that had a significant impact on its economy. Rising oil costs, a drop in worldwide demand for Pakistani goods, and political unrest in neighboring Afghanistan were among them.

Despite these obstacles, Pakistan's economy grew throughout the 1990s and early 2000s, owing in part to economic reforms adopted by successive governments. However, the country also faced internal issues such as political instability, corruption, and a lack of investment in critical areas such as education and infrastructure.

Pakistan's economy has encountered significant hurdles in recent years, including rising inflation, a large fiscal deficit, and a low foreign exchange reserve. These difficulties have resulted in a period of economic volatility, making it difficult for the country to achieve sustained economic progress.

II. The Economic Crisis

A. Definition of the Crisis

Pakistan's present economic crisis refers to a period of continuous economic turmoil and volatility that the country has experienced in recent years. A variety of interconnected concerns characterize this crisis, including high inflation, limited foreign exchange reserves, a significant fiscal deficit, and a low growth rate.

These challenges have had a substantial impact on the country's economy and citizens' lives. They have caused the cost of living to rise, the value of the currency to fall, and business confidence to fall. The crisis has also made it harder for the administration to put policies in place that promote economic growth and development.

While the crisis has several underlying causes, including structural flaws within the economy and external influences such as global economic trends and regional political instability, it is mostly the product of bad economic management and governance. The failure of the government to adopt effective economic policies, eradicate corruption, and improve the business climate has exacerbated the crisis and made it impossible for the country to solve its underlying concerns.

B. The Impact of the Crisis

Pakistan's present economic crisis has had a huge impact on the country and its people. The following are some of the most significant ways in which the crisis has impacted the country:

1. Inflation: One of the most serious consequences of the economic crisis has been an increase in inflation. The cost of life for regular residents has risen as a result, making it difficult for them to purchase basic essentials like as food, shelter, and healthcare.

2. Unemployment: As firms struggle to stay afloat and are forced to lay off workers, the economic crisis has resulted in an increase in unemployment. This has had a disproportionately negative impact on young people, who are disproportionately affected by unemployment.

3. Currency depreciation: The crisis has caused the Pakistani rupee to fall significantly in value. Imports have become more expensive as a result, raising the cost of goods and services. It has also made importing required materials and equipment more challenging for firms.

4. Reduced foreign investment: Pakistan's ability to attract international investment has been hampered by the economic crisis. This has hampered the country's ability to build critical sectors and infrastructure, as well as its ability to create new jobs and boost economic growth.

5. Social unrest: The country's social unrest has been exacerbated by the economic crisis, as citizens have grown increasingly disillusioned

with the government's inability to address their economic issues. This has sparked rallies and demonstrations, further destabilizing the country.

Overall, Pakistan's economic crisis has had a huge impact on the country and its people. It has harmed the government's ability to handle critical economic concerns, and many Pakistanis are struggling to make ends meet.

C. The Causes of the Crisis

The current economic crisis in Pakistan has several root reasons, which can be broadly classified as follows:

1. Economic structural issues: Pakistan's economy has a variety of fundamental issues that have led to the crisis. These include a large reliance on agriculture and textiles, a lack of investment in critical industries and infrastructure, and a low tax collection rate.

2. Poor economic management: The government's poor economic management has compounded the crisis, including a lack of fiscal discipline, corruption, and a failure to adopt effective economic policies.

1. Foreign issues: A number of foreign factors have impacted Pakistan, contributing to the crisis. These include rising oil costs, a drop in global demand for Pakistani products, and regional political instability.

2. Security problems: In recent years, Pakistan has faced a number of security challenges, including terrorist attacks and political instability. These difficulties have made it difficult for the

government to attract foreign investment, resulting in a drop in corporate confidence.

3. Natural calamities: Finally, Pakistan has been hit by a number of natural disasters, such as floods and droughts. These calamities have had a considerable economic impact on the country, notably on the agriculture sector.

Overall, the roots of Pakistan's economic problems are complicated and numerous. They represent both internal and external issues, and addressing them will necessitate a comprehensive and ongoing effort.

III. The Historical Context

1. The Early Years

To comprehend Pakistan's current economic problem, it is necessary to first explore the historical framework and early years of the country's economy. Pakistan gained independence from British domination in 1947, and the country experienced a variety of economic hurdles in its early years.

Pakistan gained independence with a predominantly agricultural economy and inadequate infrastructure and industrial growth. The country also faced tremendous political and social obstacles, such as mass migration of millions of people during India's and Pakistan's partition, as well as ongoing tensions with India over disputed regions.

Pakistan relied largely on foreign funding to support its economic development in its early years. The country's economy, on the other hand, increased at a relatively modest pace, and the advantages of economic expansion were not evenly dispersed. As a result, there has been tremendous social and economic inequality, as well as political instability.

With international aid and investment, Pakistan made some headway in establishing vital industries and infrastructure during the 1950s and 1960s. However, their attempts were delayed by a variety of obstacles, including corruption, inefficiencies in the bureaucracy, and a lack of efficient economic policies.

Pakistan had a period of political insecurity and economic collapse in the 1970s. A series of military governments dominated the country, characterized by corruption, inefficiency, and a lack of commitment to economic growth.

Inflation skyrocketed, foreign reserves depleted, and social unrest grew.

Pakistan began to enjoy economic growth in the 1980s, owing largely to increased investment from Gulf countries and foreign help from Western powers. However, this expansion was mostly powered by a construction boom, which was not long-term sustainable.

Overall, the early years of Pakistan's economy were fraught with difficulties and setbacks. The country's economy progressed slowly, and the benefits of economic growth were not evenly dispersed. In addition, the country had enormous political and social issues, which impeded economic development. These causes paved the way for Pakistan's current economic catastrophe.

B. The Bhutto Era

Zulfikar Ali Bhutto was a famous Pakistani politician who served as the country's Prime Minister from 1973 until 1977. Bhutto's tenure is seen as a watershed moment in Pakistan's economic and political development, and it had a considerable impact on the country's economy.

During his presidency, Bhutto implemented a series of economic reforms aimed at eliminating social and economic inequality in the country. These included nationalizing important industries like as banking and insurance, as well as boosting government spending on social welfare programmes such as education and healthcare.

Bhutto's nationalization initiatives were divisive and controversial, drawing strong resistance from business leaders and rich elites. They were, however, viewed as an important step towards eliminating economic inequality and fostering more economic opportunities for all Pakistanis.

Despite these attempts, Bhutto's economic policies were not wholly successful, and the country faced serious economic difficulties. Inflation and unemployment remained high, and political unrest persisted.

During Bhutto's reign, major geographical discrepancies within Pakistan emerged. In terms of economic development, the country's western regions, notably Balochistan and Khyber Pakhtunkhwa, lagged behind, while the eastern province of Punjab enjoyed tremendous progress.

Overall, Bhutto's presidency was a watershed moment in Pakistan's economic and political progress. While his economic policies were not always successful, they did lay the groundwork for future efforts to alleviate the country's social and economic inequalities. However, his presidency was also marked by persistent political and economic issues, which laid the groundwork for future instability and crises.

C. The Zia Years

General Zia-ul-Haq seized power in Pakistan in a military coup in 1977, when Prime Minister Zulfikar Ali Bhutto was deposed. Zia's presidency of Pakistan lasted until his death in 1988, and he had a major impact on the country's economic and political progress.

During his presidency, Zia implemented an economic liberalization programme that included decreasing government regulation and encouraging private sector investment. This programme was conceived as a response to the economic stagnation that had characterized Pakistan's economy during the preceding decade, with the goal of promoting more economic growth and development.

In certain ways, Zia's economic initiatives were successful. During the 1980s, the country experienced substantial economic expansion, fueled in part by increased investment from Gulf countries and foreign aid from the United States. Construction, in particular, had tremendous growth, spurred by increased investment in infrastructure projects.

Zia's economic initiatives, however, had some unfavorable results. Economic liberalization boosted inequality and widened the wealth gap between affluent and poor. The government's emphasis on boosting the private sector has resulted in a disregard for public sector investment in critical areas such as education and healthcare.

Zia's presidency was also marred by persistent political and societal unrest. The country was highly split along ethnic, religious, and political lines, and there was widespread instability and violence. Zia's assistance for the Afghan mujahedeen in their fight against Soviet forces exacerbated Pakistan's instability and turmoil.

Overall, Pakistan's economic and political landscape changed dramatically during the Zia administration. While Zia's economic policies brought to some growth and progress, they also contributed to persistent economic disparity and the neglect of critical social services. The country also faced severe political and social issues, laying the groundwork for future instability and conflict.

D. The Return of Democracy

Pakistan reverted to democracy after the death of General Zia-ul-Haq in 1988, with a new constitution and national elections. During this time, the Pakistan People's Party (PPP) and its leader, Benazir Bhutto, the daughter of previous Prime Minister Zulfikar Ali Bhutto, rose to prominence.

The early years of democracy saw some advances in economic and social growth. Benazir Bhutto's government implemented a variety of policies aimed at decreasing poverty and encouraging economic growth. Increased investment in infrastructure and social welfare programmes, as well as initiatives to encourage foreign investment and trade, were among them.

However, these advantages were fleeting, and the country rapidly descended into political and economic chaos. President Ghulam Ishaq Khan dismissed Benazir Bhutto's cabinet in 1990 due to allegations of corruption and inefficiency.

The years that followed saw a series of short-lived governments, frequent leadership changes, and persistent political instability. With high inflation and an increasing debt issue, the country's economy also faltered.

In 1999, the military seized control of the government once more, with General Pervez Musharraf leading a coup. Musharraf's presidency witnessed some economic and social development improvements, but it was also defined by persistent political and social instability, as well as charges of human rights violations.

Overall, Pakistan's economic and political development was mixed following the return of democracy in the late 1980s. While there were modest achievements in terms of economic growth and social welfare, political insecurity and corruption continued to stymie long-term progress. This paved the way for future economic and political crises, which would have serious consequences for the country's progress.

IV. The Current Economic Landscape

A. GDP and Growth

In recent years, Pakistan's economy has faced considerable challenges, with poor growth rates and severe structural issues contributing to a chronic economic crisis.

In terms of GDP, Pakistan's economy has risen at a rate of roughly 2-3% per year on average during the last decade, much below the country's long-term growth potential. A number of factors have contributed to this, including continued political insecurity, security worries, and structural challenges such as a lack of investment in vital sectors.

The epidemic of COVID-19 has also had a substantial influence on Pakistan's economy, with GDP growth dropping by 0.5% in fiscal year 2020-21. The pandemic has been especially severe for the country's export-oriented businesses, with a dramatic drop in demand for textiles and other items. The government has launched a variety of economic stimulus measures, including a relief package for small enterprises and low-income households, but their impact has been limited.

One of the most pressing issues confronting Pakistan's economy is a lack of investment in critical sectors such as infrastructure and human capital. The country's infrastructure is antiquated and insufficient, with poor transportation and power supply producing substantial economic bottlenecks. Furthermore, the country's education system is underdeveloped, with a lack of human capital investment contributing to a skilled labour shortage and a low-quality labour force.

Agriculture remains a key contributor to Pakistan's economy, accounting for approximately 19% of GDP and employing over 38% of the labour force. However, the sector confronts considerable obstacles, including as water scarcity, inadequate infrastructure, and low production.

The industrial sector contributes significantly to the economy, accounting for approximately 20% of GDP. However, the sector has been heavily damaged by the COVID-19 epidemic, with a drop in export demand and persistent energy supply concerns adding to a lack of growth.

Overall, Pakistan's economic landscape remains difficult, with persisting difficulties such as political insecurity, security worries, and structural issues all contributing to a lack of sustainable economic progress. The country confronts tremendous hurdles in terms of infrastructure development, human capital investment, and key sector reform, all of which must be addressed in order to achieve long-term economic growth and development.

B. Inflation and Interest Rates

Inflation and interest rates are important markers of an economy's health, and both have been serious worries in Pakistan in recent years.

Over the last decade, Pakistan has seen severe inflation, with average annual inflation rates of roughly 7-8%. A combination of factors has contributed to this, including high levels of government borrowing, a lack of investment in critical areas like as agriculture and energy, and external shocks such as the global spike in commodity prices.

Inflationary pressures have increased the cost of living for regular Pakistanis, particularly those on low salaries. Rising food and gasoline prices have imposed a considerable strain on people, sparking major protests and social instability.

The government has tried a variety of methods to combat inflation, including tightening monetary policy and raising interest rates. These policies, however, have had limited success, with inflation remaining stubbornly high.

In Pakistan, interest rates have been a key source of concern in recent years, with the State Bank of Pakistan (SBP) boosting rates dramatically to battle inflation. In an attempt to manage inflation and stabilize the economy, the SBP raised its policy rate to 13.25% in 2019, one of the highest in the world.

High interest rates, on the other hand, have had a substantial impact on Pakistan's businesses and households, making borrowing money more expensive and inhibiting economic progress. Borrowing costs have also contributed to a lack of investment in critical sectors such as infrastructure and human resources.

Overall, inflation and interest rates continue to be major concerns for the Pakistani economy. To solve these concerns, the government will need to pursue a variety of measures, including increased investment in important sectors, stricter fiscal policy, and banking system reform.

C. Fiscal Deficit and Public Debt

Pakistan's economy is facing two key challenges: fiscal deficit and public debt.

The fiscal deficit is the gap between the revenue and spending of the government. Over the last decade, Pakistan's fiscal deficit has been large, averaging around 5-6% of GDP. A variety of factors have contributed to this, including poor tax collections, high levels of government borrowing, and a lack of fiscal discipline.

The country's massive fiscal deficit has had a number of detrimental effects on the economy. As a result, the government has been compelled to borrow to support its spending, which has resulted in a significant increase in national debt. It has also strained the country's external finances, since the government has had to borrow from overseas lenders to cover the deficit.

Pakistan's public debt has climbed quickly in recent years, from over 60% of GDP in 2013 to more than 90% in 2021. The country's high level of debt has put enormous strain on its fiscal and external accounts, limiting the government's capacity to invest in critical sectors such as infrastructure and human capital.

The government has tried a variety of methods to alleviate the fiscal deficit and public debt, including tax reforms, subsidy reductions, and revenue increases through privatization. However, progress has been slow, and Pakistan's economy continues to face substantial hurdles due to the massive fiscal imbalance and public debt.

To overcome these concerns, the government will need to enact more substantial changes, such as more fiscal discipline, enhanced tax collection, and a reduction in wasteful spending. The government will also need to address the underlying reasons of the deficit, such as a lack of investment in critical sectors and the need for improved efficiency in government spending.

D. Foreign Exchange Reserves and Exchange Rate

Foreign exchange reserves and currency rates are crucial indications of Pakistan's economic health.

The amount of foreign currency kept by the State Bank of Pakistan (SBP) and other authorized financial institutions is referred to as foreign exchange reserves. These reserves are used to finance foreign trade and investment, as well as to support the country's currency's value.

With a prolonged current account deficit, Pakistan's foreign exchange reserves have been a source of concern in recent years. As a result, the country's reserves have fallen to critically low levels in 2018. However, in recent years, the government has taken a number of steps to solve this issue, including borrowing from foreign lenders and obtaining aid from friendly countries like as China and Saudi Arabia. As a result, Pakistan's foreign exchange reserves have grown dramatically in recent years, reaching over $18 billion.

The value of one currency in respect to another is referred to as the exchange rate. In Pakistan, market forces govern the currency rate, with the State Bank of Pakistan intervening only in extreme instances to avoid substantial changes.

In recent years, Pakistan has encountered considerable issues with its exchange rate, with the value of the Pakistani rupee steadily dropping versus the US dollar. A number of factors have contributed to this, including the country's ongoing current account deficit, high levels of public debt, and a lack of investor confidence. However, the government has taken a number of steps to address this problem in recent years, including hiking interest rates, tightening monetary policy, and strengthening foreign exchange reserves. As a result, the Pakistani rupee's value has stabilized in recent years, while it remains susceptible to foreign shocks.

Foreign exchange reserves and currency rates are crucial indications of Pakistan's economic health. To maintain the economy's long-term stability and growth, the government must continue to pursue measures that support the country's reserves and stabilize its currency rate.

V. The Role of Agriculture

A. Overview of Agriculture in Pakistan

Agriculture is an important sector of the Pakistani economy, accounting for approximately 20% of the country's GDP and employing over 42% of the workforce. Agriculture exports account for over 10% of total exports, making it a significant source of foreign exchange earnings.

Wheat, rice, cotton, sugarcane, maize, and pulses are the most important crops farmed in Pakistan. Livestock is another key sub-sector, with Pakistan ranking fifth in the world in terms of milk production. The country is also a large producer of fruits and vegetables, with mangoes, citrus fruits, and onions among the most important crops.

Despite its importance, the agricultural sector faces a number of obstacles. Water shortages, low productivity, and restricted access to contemporary technology and infrastructure are among them. Furthermore, the sector is sensitive to climate change, with shifting weather patterns and an increase in the frequency of extreme weather events such as floods and droughts affecting crop yields and livestock output.

To address these difficulties, the government has established a number of laws and initiatives targeted at increasing agricultural output and sustainability. Investments in irrigation infrastructure, research and development in new crop types and agricultural practices, and assistance to small farmers through programmes such as the Benazir Income Support Programme are examples of these.

Despite these efforts, much more has to be done to fully realize Pakistan's agriculture sector's potential. The government must continue to invest in infrastructure, research, and technology while simultaneously tackling the root causes of water scarcity and climate change. In this way, the country may enhance its agricultural sector while also contributing to long-term economic growth and development.

B. Issues with Agriculture

Despite its importance to the Pakistani economy, the agricultural sector faces a number of obstacles that have hampered its growth and development. Some of the major difficulties confronting agriculture in Pakistan are as follows:

1. Water Scarcity: Pakistan is experiencing a severe water scarcity crisis, with per capita water availability declining dramatically in recent years. This has had a significant impact on the agriculture industry, which is primarily reliant on irrigation to produce crops. As a result, farmers are experiencing lower yields and higher costs, while also dealing with water issues and tensions.

2. Low Productivity: Pakistan's agricultural sector's productivity is rather low, with yields per hectare falling short of international benchmarks. This is due, in part, to a lack of contemporary technology and infrastructure, as well as limited access to loans and inputs and inadequate extension services.

3. Climate Change: Pakistan is extremely sensitive to the effects of climate change, with changing weather patterns and catastrophic weather events like floods and droughts wreaking havoc on crop yields and livestock productivity. This has made crop planning and management more complicated for farmers, as well as increasing risks and expenses.

4. Limited Financial Access: Many small-scale farmers in Pakistan struggle to obtain finance and credit, limiting their capacity to invest in modern technologies and inputs. This has also led to a lack of investment in the agricultural sector as a whole, impeding its growth and development.

5. Lack of Research and Development: Limited investment in agricultural research and development in Pakistan has resulted in a lack of innovation and delayed progress in solving the sector's difficulties. This has also constrained farmers' ability to adopt new technologies and practices that could boost yields and productivity.

To address these concerns, considerable investments in infrastructure, technology, and research will be required, as well as policy reforms that helps small farmers and promotes sustainable farming practices. Pakistan can boost its agriculture industry while also contributing to long-term economic growth and development.

C. Possible Solutions

To address the issues confronting Pakistan's agricultural industry, a variety of policies and programmes aiming at enhancing production, sustainability, and resilience will be required. Among the possible solutions are:

1. Water Conservation and Management: The government can invest in water conservation and management measures such as dam construction, irrigation infrastructure improvements, and the promotion of water-efficient technologies and practices. This will help to boost water availability and improve agriculture sector sustainability.

2. Technology and Innovation: The government can encourage the use of innovative technologies and practices that increase production while lowering costs, such as precision agriculture, drip irrigation, and mechanization. The government can also spend in R&D to aid in the creation of new crop types and better management practices.

3. Small Farmer Support: The government can put laws and programmes in place to help small-scale farmers, such as providing access to finance and credit, strengthening extension services, and supporting cooperatives and producer organizations. This will help to guarantee that small farmers get the resources and assistance they require to invest in their farms and increase output.

4. Climate Change Adaptation: The government may assist farmers adapt to the effects of climate change by producing drought-resistant crop types, improving

water management, and encouraging sustainable land management practices. This will help to strengthen the agricultural sector's resilience and lower the risk of crop failures and losses.

5. Market Access and Export Promotion: By developing infrastructure, lowering trade obstacles, and promoting Pakistan's agricultural products in foreign markets, the government may improve market access and export promotion for agricultural products. This would help to enhance demand for agricultural products in Pakistan and raise the sector's contribution to the country's economy.

Pakistan may boost its agriculture industry and achieve long-term economic growth and development by following these and other measures.

VI. The Manufacturing Sector

A. Overview of Manufacturing in Pakistan

Manufacturing is a significant sector of the Pakistani economy, accounting for approximately 13% of the country's GDP and employing approximately 20% of the labour force. Textiles, food processing, pharmaceuticals, chemicals, cement, steel, and vehicles are among the industries that make up the manufacturing sector.

The textile industry is the largest sub-sector of the manufacturing sector, accounting for over 60% of total exports and employing a sizable share of the labour force. Pakistan is the world's fourth-largest cotton grower, with a thriving textile industry that has profited from government incentives and assistance.

Another important sub-sector of manufacturing is food processing, with Pakistan having a varied range of agricultural goods that can be turned into value-added products. Other important manufacturing sub-sectors include the pharmaceuticals business, which is quickly expanding due to increased demand for medications, and the chemicals industry, which manufactures a variety of products such as fertilizers, plastics, and dyes.

Despite its importance to the Pakistani economy, the manufacturing sector faces a number of obstacles that have hampered its growth and development. These difficulties include limited access to funding, inadequate infrastructure, a skilled labour scarcity, and a challenging business environment.

To overcome these problems, the government has established a number of policies and initiatives targeted at supporting manufacturing sector growth and development. These include incentives and assistance for export-oriented sectors, improved access to capital and credit, infrastructure investment, and promotion of technical and vocational education and training.

Overall, the manufacturing sector has the potential to contribute significantly to Pakistan's economic growth and development; but, it will require ongoing investment and governmental assistance to address the issues it faces and realize its full potential.

B. Issues with Manufacturing

While manufacturing is an important sector of the Pakistani economy, it is confronted with a number of obstacles that have hampered its growth and development. Some of Pakistan's key manufacturing concerns include:

1. Inadequate Infrastructure: Pakistan's manufacturing industry is impeded by inadequate infrastructure, which includes a lack of reliable electricity, weak transportation networks, and a lack of modern ports and airports. This limits manufacturers' capacity to deliver goods efficiently and effectively, which can raise costs and impair competitiveness.

2. Limited Access to Finance: Pakistani manufacturers frequently struggle to obtain the financing they require to invest in new equipment, technology, and facilities. This is due, in part, to a scarcity of financing sources, high interest rates, and a challenging business environment.

3. Skilled Labour deficit: The manufacturing sector in Pakistan also confronts a skilled labour deficit, making it difficult for businesses to locate personnel with the requisite technical and managerial abilities. This can reduce productivity and competitiveness, as well as raise labour costs as businesses are obliged to pay greater rates to recruit qualified personnel.

4. Ineffective Regulatory Environment: The regulatory environment in Pakistan is frequently identified as a major obstacle to the expansion of the industrial industry. Regulations can be complex, inconsistent, and difficult to manage, causing producers to incur additional expenses and administrative constraints.

5. Energy Crisis: The manufacturing industry in Pakistan is strongly reliant on energy, with electricity and natural gas being the most critical inputs. The country,

however, has been experiencing an energy crisis, with regular power outages and shortages. This has had a tremendous influence on the sector, resulting in decreased production and increased prices.

Addressing these difficulties would necessitate a variety of policies and efforts targeted at strengthening infrastructure, increasing access to finance, investing in skill development, improving the regulatory environment, and dealing with the energy crisis. Pakistan may boost its manufacturing industry and achieve long-term economic growth and development by tackling these concerns.

C. Possible Solutions

A variety of remedies can be applied to alleviate the difficulties confronting Pakistan's manufacturing sector, including:

1. Improving Infrastructure: The government can invest in the creation and upkeep of modern ports, airports, and transportation networks to address the issue of inadequate infrastructure. This can help to cut transportation costs, improve efficiency, and boost competitiveness.

2. Promoting Access to Finance: To address the issue of limited access to finance, the government can work to create a more supportive financial environment by lowering interest rates, encouraging venture capital investment, and encouraging the establishment of more credit institutions that serve the needs of small and medium-sized businesses (SMEs).

3. Investing in Skills Development: To address the issue of a skilled labour shortage, the government might invest

in skill development programmes that provide technical and managerial training. This can help to build a pool of skilled individuals to help the manufacturing industry grow.

4. Streamlining the Regulatory Environment: The government can seek to simplify regulations and minimize bureaucracy in order to solve the issue of an inefficient regulatory environment. This can help to minimize administrative costs and make the atmosphere more business-friendly.

5. Addressing the Energy problem: To address the energy problem, the government can invest in new power plants and increase the usage of renewable energy sources to help cut demand, the government might also act to reduce energy subsidies and promote energy conservation measures.

Overcoming the difficulties plaguing Pakistan's manufacturing industry would require a collective effort involving the government, private sector, and civil society. By implementing the guidelines outlined above, Pakistan can enhance its manufacturing sector and achieve long-term economic growth and development.

<u>VII. The Services Sector</u>

A. Overview of Services in Pakistan

The services sector is the largest in Pakistan's economy, accounting for more than 60% of GDP and employing more than 50% of the workforce. Telecommunications, financial services, transportation, wholesale and retail trade, and hospitality and tourism are all part of the sector.

1. Telecommunications: The telecommunications sector is one of Pakistan's fastest-growing businesses, owing to increased demand for mobile services and internet access. Pakistan Telecommunication Company Limited (PTCL), Mobilink, and Telenor are among the industry's major players.

2. Financial Services: Another prominent industry in Pakistan is the financial services sector, which includes banks, insurance companies, and stock exchanges. The State Bank of Pakistan regulates the sector, and key companies include National Bank of Pakistan, Habib Bank Limited, and United Bank Limited.

3. Transportation: The transportation sector in Pakistan is varied, offering both domestic and international services. With nearly 260,000 km of road, the country has a substantial road network, as well as a railway network that connects key cities. The national carrier is Pakistan International Airlines, and the country's ports and airports serve as significant regional commercial hubs.

4. Wholesale and retail trade is a major component of Pakistan's economy, and it encompasses a wide range

of businesses, from local neighborhood shops to large chain stores. Metro Cash & Carry, Carrefour, and Al-Fatah are among the major participants in the market.

5. Hospitality and Tourism: The hospitality and tourism industry in Pakistan is expanding, with a wide range of attractions such as historical monuments, cultural events, and natural beauty. The ancient city of Taxila, the picturesque Swat Valley, and the hilly northern regions are all popular tourist sites.

Overall, the services industry is an important part of Pakistan's economy, providing a variety of job and business opportunities. However, the sector has a number of problems, such as a lack of infrastructure and technology investment, restricted access to funding, and a tough regulatory environment. To address these difficulties, a variety of policies and programmes targeted at stimulating investment, streamlining regulations, and promoting innovation and growth will be required.

B. Issues with Services

In Pakistan, the services sector has a number of problems that impede its growth and development. Among the significant difficulties confronting the sector are:

1. Inadequate Infrastructure Investment: Pakistan's services sector suffers from inadequate infrastructure, particularly transportation, communication, and energy. This impedes service delivery, reduces service quality, and raises service costs.

2. Limited Access to funding: Many service providers in Pakistan, particularly small and medium-sized firms (SMEs), struggle to obtain funding. This constrains their

capacity to invest in their companies, develop their technology, and extend their offerings.

3. **Difficulty in Doing Business:** The services sector in Pakistan faces a range of regulatory hurdles that make it difficult to do business. The process of obtaining licenses and permits is time-consuming and expensive, and bureaucratic red tape can limit innovation and growth.

4. **Skills Gap:** The skills of the workforce in the services sector are frequently insufficient, particularly for low-skilled workers. This has the potential to reduce the quality of services supplied and stifle the sector's growth.

Many service providers in Pakistan continue to rely on old methods of service delivery, with little use of contemporary technologies. This reduces service efficiency and quality, as well as the sector's capacity to compete in a globalized market.

Addressing these difficulties will necessitate a variety of policy initiatives, such as infrastructural investments, expanding access to finance, reducing laws, investing in talent development, and encouraging the use of new technologies. By tackling these issues, Pakistan's services sector can achieve improved efficiency, quality, and competitiveness, hence boosting growth and development.

C. Possible Solutions

Several policy actions can be implemented to solve the issues confronting Pakistan's services sector. Among the possible solutions are:

1. Infrastructure Investment: The government can invest in infrastructure development, such as transportation, communication, and energy, to improve service delivery, reduce costs, and improve quality.

2. Access to funding: Through measures like as credit guarantees, risk-sharing structures, and subsidies, the government can increase access to funding for service providers, particularly SMEs. Service providers will be able to invest in their operations, modernize their technology, and extend their offerings as a result of this.

3. Streamlining Regulations: The government can simplify and streamline regulations to make doing business easier for service providers. This can be accomplished by decreasing bureaucracy, simplifying licensing procedures, and offering online application and payment platforms.

4. Skills Development: Through measures such as vocational training programmes, apprenticeships, and education and training programmes, the government can invest in the development of workforce skills in the services sector. This would improve service quality while also promoting sector growth.

5. Technology Adoption: The government can stimulate the use of modern technology in the services sector by measures such as tax breaks, subsidies, and grants for technology purchases. This will increase the efficiency and quality of services while also increasing the sector's competitiveness.

In addition to these legislative measures, it is critical to address broader issues like as corruption, political insecurity, and security concerns, all of which can have an impact on the investment climate and the expansion of the services sector. Pakistan may attain higher efficiency, quality, and competitiveness in the services industry by solving these difficulties and establishing a favorable investment climate, hence boosting growth and development.

VIII. Trade and Investment

A. Overview of Trade and Investment in Pakistan

Trade and investment play a critical role in Pakistan's economy. The country is strategically located at the crossroads of South Asia, Central Asia, and the Middle East, making it a gateway to these regions. Pakistan has a diverse economy, with a range of sectors that offer investment opportunities to foreign investors.

Pakistan's main exports include textiles and clothing, leather goods, rice, fruits, and vegetables, while its major imports include oil, machinery, chemicals, and vehicles. Pakistan's major trading partners include China, the United States, the United Kingdom, and the United Arab Emirates.

Foreign investment in Pakistan has been growing in recent years, with significant investments in sectors such as energy, infrastructure, telecommunications, and manufacturing. The government has taken steps to improve the investment climate, including streamlining regulations, providing incentives, and improving infrastructure.

Despite the growth in foreign investment, Pakistan faces several challenges in attracting more investment and expanding its trade. These challenges include political instability, security concerns, corruption, inadequate infrastructure, and bureaucratic hurdles.

To address these challenges, the government has taken several steps to improve the investment climate, including establishing special economic zones, offering tax incentives, and simplifying regulations. The government has also prioritized investment in infrastructure, including the development of transportation networks, energy infrastructure, and communication systems.

Overall, trade and investment are critical to Pakistan's economy, providing employment opportunities, driving growth and development, and contributing to the country's integration into the global economy.

B. Issues with Trade and Investment

Pakistan faces several challenges in attracting investment and expanding its trade, including:

1. Political instability: Pakistan has faced political instability in the past, which has contributed to a lack of investor confidence. Political uncertainty, such as changes in government, can create uncertainty and risk for foreign investors.

2. Security concerns: Pakistan has been affected by terrorism and political violence, which has led to security concerns for investors. The security situation in the country has improved in recent years, but incidents of violence still occur.

3. Corruption: Corruption is a major challenge in Pakistan, which can create a difficult business environment for foreign investors. The government has taken steps to address corruption, but more needs to be done to

improve transparency and accountability.

4. Inadequate infrastructure: Pakistan's infrastructure is underdeveloped, which can create logistical challenges for businesses. The country lacks modern transportation networks, energy infrastructure, and communication systems.

5. Bureaucratic hurdles: Pakistan's bureaucracy can be slow and inefficient, which can create challenges for businesses trying to navigate regulatory requirements.

6. Lack of skilled workforce: Pakistan has a shortage of skilled workers, which can make it difficult for businesses to find qualified employees. This can be a particular challenge in industries that require specialized skills, such as technology and engineering.

Addressing these challenges will require a concerted effort from the government, private sector, and civil society. The government can take steps to improve the investment climate by reducing corruption, streamlining regulations, and investing in infrastructure. The private sector can also play a role by investing in training and education programs to develop the skills of the workforce. Finally, civil society can advocate for greater transparency and accountability, and encourage the government to take action to address these challenges.

C. Possible Solutions

To address the challenges facing trade and investment in Pakistan, several possible solutions can be considered:

1. Political stability: The government can take steps to ensure political stability, such as promoting a stable political environment and creating policies that support long-term economic growth.

2. Security: The government can continue to invest in security measures to ensure the safety of foreign investors and create a more stable environment for investment.

3. Corruption: The government can take action to address corruption by strengthening anti-corruption laws and enforcing them more effectively. The government can also work to improve transparency and accountability in public institutions.

4. Infrastructure: The government can invest in infrastructure development to create a more efficient and effective business environment. This can include investments in transportation networks, energy infrastructure, and communication systems.

5. Bureaucratic hurdles: The government can work to streamline regulatory requirements and create a more efficient bureaucracy. This can include simplifying procedures, reducing paperwork, and eliminating unnecessary regulations.

6. Skilled workforce: The government can invest in education and training programs to develop the skills of the workforce, particularly in industries that require specialized skills. This can include partnerships between the private sector and educational institutions to create targeted training programs.

7. Incentives: The government can offer incentives to foreign investors, such as tax breaks or subsidies, to encourage investment in the country.

8. Special economic zones: The government can create special economic zones with streamlined regulations and infrastructure development to attract foreign investors and encourage economic growth.

Overall, addressing the challenges facing trade and investment in Pakistan will require a multi-faceted approach that involves the government, private sector, and civil society. By taking action to promote a more stable and supportive business environment, Pakistan can attract more investment and expand its trade, leading to long-term economic growth and development.

IX. Infrastructure and Energy

A. Overview of Infrastructure and Energy in Pakistan

Pakistan faces significant challenges in its infrastructure and energy sectors, which are crucial for the country's economic development.

Infrastructure:

Pakistan's infrastructure is inadequate and underdeveloped, with poor roads, limited access to clean water, and insufficient housing. The country ranks low on the World Bank's infrastructure index, with significant disparities between urban and rural areas. Pakistan also faces challenges in maintaining existing infrastructure due to insufficient funding, inadequate maintenance, and lack of planning.

Energy:

Pakistan's energy sector faces significant challenges, including a chronic energy shortage that has resulted in frequent blackouts and load shedding. The country relies heavily on imported oil, which makes it vulnerable to price fluctuations in the international market. The electricity generation capacity is insufficient, and the transmission and distribution infrastructure is inadequate. As a result, Pakistan's energy sector is in a state of crisis, with significant economic and social consequences.

B. Possible Solutions

1. Increased investment: Pakistan needs significant investment in infrastructure to address its development challenges. This can be achieved through public-private partnerships, foreign direct investment, and other innovative financing mechanisms.

2. Improved planning and management: Infrastructure projects require detailed planning, effective management, and coordination between government agencies, private sector partners, and communities. This can be achieved through the establishment of regulatory frameworks, the strengthening of project management capacity, and the promotion of public-private partnerships.

3. Renewable energy: Pakistan has significant potential for renewable energy, including wind, solar, and hydro. The development of renewable energy can reduce Pakistan's reliance on imported oil and promote sustainable development.

4. Energy efficiency: Improving energy efficiency can help reduce energy demand and promote sustainable development. This can be achieved through the promotion of energy-efficient technologies, building codes, and energy management systems.

5. Regional cooperation: Pakistan can benefit from regional cooperation in energy and infrastructure development, including through the development of regional electricity grids, joint investment projects, and

cooperation in the development of renewable energy.

Overall, addressing the challenges in infrastructure and energy in Pakistan requires sustained investment, effective planning and management, and a commitment to promoting sustainable development.

<u>X. Education and Health</u>

A. Overview of Education and Health in Pakistan

Education and health are two critical sectors in Pakistan that have a significant impact on the country's economic and social development.

Education:

Pakistan has made significant progress in increasing access to education over the past few decades. The country has a large and growing population of school-aged children, with approximately 22.8 million enrolled in primary and secondary schools in 2019.

However, the quality of education remains a significant challenge in Pakistan. Many schools lack basic facilities, and teachers are often poorly trained and unmotivated. As a result, the learning outcomes of students are often poor, and the country has a high dropout rate.

The government of Pakistan has taken steps to improve the quality of education in recent years. These measures include increasing the education budget, providing teacher training, and implementing education reforms. However, progress has been slow, and the education system still faces significant challenges.

Health:

The health sector in Pakistan faces numerous challenges, including a shortage of health facilities, a lack of trained healthcare professionals, and inadequate funding. The country has a high burden of communicable and non-communicable diseases, and many people lack access to basic healthcare services.

Pakistan also faces significant public health challenges, including high rates of malnutrition and infant mortality. The COVID-19 pandemic has further highlighted the weaknesses in the country's health system and its lack of preparedness for a public health crisis.

The government of Pakistan has taken steps to address these challenges, such as increasing health funding and implementing health reforms. However, progress has been slow, and the health sector still faces significant challenges.

Overall, education and health are critical sectors in Pakistan that require significant investments and reforms to ensure that all citizens have access to quality education and healthcare services. Improving these sectors is crucial for the country's long-term economic and social development.

B. Issues with Education and Health

Education and health are two critical sectors in Pakistan that face significant challenges.

Education:

One of the most significant challenges facing the education sector in Pakistan is the poor quality of education. Many schools lack basic facilities such as clean water, electricity, and toilets. Teachers are often underpaid, poorly trained, and unmotivated, which leads to a high dropout rate and poor learning outcomes.

Another challenge is the lack of access to education, particularly for girls and children in rural areas. Many families in rural areas do not prioritize education for their children, and girls face cultural and social barriers to attending school. As a result, Pakistan has one of the lowest literacy rates in the world, with only around 60% of the population being able to read and write.

Health:

The health sector in Pakistan also faces significant challenges. One of the most significant challenges is a shortage of health facilities and trained healthcare professionals, particularly in rural areas. This shortage of healthcare services is further exacerbated by the inadequate funding for the health sector, which limits the government's ability to improve healthcare access and quality.

Another challenge is the high burden of communicable and non-communicable diseases, including polio, tuberculosis, hepatitis, and diabetes. The country also has a high maternal mortality rate and a high prevalence of malnutrition, which affects the health of millions of children.

The COVID-19 pandemic has further highlighted the weaknesses in the country's health system and its lack of preparedness for a public health crisis. The pandemic has also exacerbated the existing challenges facing the health sector, including the shortage of healthcare professionals, inadequate funding, and the need for better healthcare infrastructure and equipment.

Overall, improving the quality and access to education and healthcare services in Pakistan is critical for the country's long-term economic and social development. However, addressing the challenges facing these sectors requires significant investments and reforms, which will take time and resources to achieve.

C. Possible Solutions

Addressing the challenges facing education and health in Pakistan requires a multi-faceted approach that includes investments in infrastructure, human resources, and policy reforms. Some possible solutions are:

Education:

1. Improving the quality of education: The government should invest in teacher training, curriculum development, and school infrastructure to ensure that children receive a quality education. Teachers should be incentivized and motivated to provide better education to students.

2. Increasing access to education: The government should increase funding for schools and provide free education to all children. Special attention should be given to promoting girls' education, especially in rural areas where cultural barriers often prevent girls from attending school.

3. Using technology for education: The use of digital technology can help to provide quality education to students who cannot access it through traditional means. The government should invest in digital infrastructure and platforms for delivering online education.

Health:

1. Increasing healthcare funding: The government should increase funding for the health sector to improve the quality and access to healthcare services, particularly in rural areas. More healthcare facilities should be established in rural areas and existing facilities should be equipped with modern equipment.

2. Developing healthcare human resources: The government should invest in the training and development of healthcare professionals, including doctors, nurses, and other support staff. This will help to address the shortage of healthcare professionals in the country.

3. Promoting preventive healthcare: The government should promote public awareness of preventive healthcare measures, including vaccination campaigns, health education programs, and nutrition interventions. This will help to reduce the burden of communicable and non-communicable diseases in the country.

4. Improving emergency preparedness: The COVID-19 pandemic has exposed the weaknesses in Pakistan's health system, particularly in emergency preparedness. The government should invest in strengthening the health system's capacity to respond to emergencies and pandemics, including developing stockpiles of essential medical supplies and equipment.

Overall, addressing the challenges facing education and healthcare in Pakistan requires significant investments in infrastructure, human resources, and policy reforms. However, if these challenges are addressed, they can have a significant impact on the country's long-term economic and social development.

XI. Governance and Corruption

A. Overview of Governance and Corruption in Pakistan

Governance and corruption are significant challenges in Pakistan. The country has struggled with poor governance and endemic corruption for many years, which has had a negative impact on economic growth, social development, and political stability.

Pakistan's governance structures are characterized by weak institutions, ineffective policies, and a lack of transparency and accountability. The government has failed to establish effective mechanisms for delivering public services, enforcing the rule of law, and promoting good governance. The judicial system is slow, under-resourced, and often subject to political influence. As a result, citizens often face significant challenges in accessing justice and enforcing their rights.

Corruption is also a major issue in Pakistan, affecting both the public and private sectors. Corruption is pervasive in government institutions, and public officials are often involved in illegal activities such as embezzlement, bribery, and kickbacks. Corruption also undermines the functioning of the private sector by increasing the cost of doing business, limiting competition, and creating an uneven playing field.

The impact of governance and corruption on the economy is significant. Corruption discourages foreign investment and undermines the credibility of government policies. Weak governance structures reduce the effectiveness of public services, including education, health, and infrastructure, which limits economic growth and social development.

Addressing the governance and corruption challenges in Pakistan requires a multi-pronged approach, including policy reforms, institutional strengthening, and public awareness campaigns. Some possible solutions are:

1. Establishing independent accountability institutions: The government should establish independent anti-corruption institutions and empower them to investigate and prosecute corruption cases.

2. Enhancing transparency and accountability: The government should promote transparency and accountability by introducing measures such as public disclosure of assets, budgets, and government contracts.

3. Improving public service delivery: The government should improve public service delivery by investing in human resources, infrastructure, and technology. This will help to reduce opportunities for corruption and improve the effectiveness of public services.

4. Promoting public awareness: The government should promote public awareness of corruption and its impact on the economy and society. This can be done through education and awareness campaigns, as well as by providing channels for citizens to report corruption.

Overall, addressing governance and corruption challenges in Pakistan is essential for promoting economic growth, social development, and political stability. It requires sustained efforts on the part of the government, civil society, and the private sector to establish effective governance structures and promote a culture of transparency and accountability.

B. Issues with Governance and Corruption

There are numerous issues with governance and corruption in Pakistan. Some of the key issues are:

1. Weak institutions: Pakistan's institutions, including the judiciary, police, and civil service, are weak and often lack the capacity to enforce the rule of law and deliver public services effectively.

2. Political interference: Political interference in government institutions is a common problem in Pakistan. This can undermine the independence of institutions and create opportunities for corruption.

3. Lack of transparency and accountability: There is a lack of transparency and accountability in government decision-making and spending. This creates opportunities for corruption and reduces public trust in government institutions.

4. Patronage networks: Patronage networks, where politicians and bureaucrats distribute public resources and jobs to their supporters, are a significant source of corruption in Pakistan.

5. Informal economy: A large portion of Pakistan's economy is informal, which can create opportunities for corruption and tax evasion.

6. Money laundering: Pakistan has been identified as a high-risk country for money laundering, which can be facilitated by weak governance and corruption.

7. Lack of public trust: Low levels of public trust in government institutions can lead to social and political

instability, which can further undermine economic development.

8. Gender inequality: Women in Pakistan often face barriers to accessing justice and public services, which can exacerbate corruption and undermine gender equality.

These issues with governance and corruption have a significant impact on the economy and society in Pakistan. They reduce the effectiveness of public services, undermine investor confidence, and limit opportunities for economic growth and social development. Addressing these issues requires sustained efforts to strengthen institutions, promote transparency and accountability, and reduce opportunities for corruption.

C. Possible Solutions

Addressing the issues of governance and corruption in Pakistan requires a multi-pronged approach. Some possible solutions include:

1. Strengthening institutions: This can be done by increasing the capacity of government institutions, improving recruitment and training processes, and promoting the independence of institutions from political interference.

2. Promoting transparency and accountability: This can be achieved through measures such as open budgeting, public procurement reforms, and increasing access to information.

3. Tackling patronage networks: This can be done through merit-based recruitment, reducing discretionary powers, and strengthening oversight mechanisms.

4. Formalizing the informal economy: This can be achieved through measures such as simplifying tax regimes, promoting entrepreneurship, and reducing regulatory barriers.

5. Combating money laundering: This can be done by strengthening the capacity of financial institutions and law enforcement agencies, improving regulations, and increasing international cooperation.

6. Building public trust: This requires measures such as promoting access to justice and public services, strengthening human rights protections, and increasing citizen participation in governance.

7. Addressing gender inequality: This requires measures such as improving access to justice and services for women, promoting women's political participation, and strengthening laws and policies that promote gender equality.

Overall, addressing the issues of governance and corruption in Pakistan requires sustained political will, strong leadership, and a commitment to transparency, accountability, and the rule of law.

XII. Conclusion

A. Summary of Findings

Pakistan is facing a severe economic crisis characterized by high inflation, fiscal deficit, public debt, low foreign exchange reserves, and weak economic growth. The crisis is rooted in various structural issues such as low productivity, inadequate infrastructure, energy crisis, weak governance, corruption, and political instability.

The agriculture sector, which employs the majority of the population, suffers from low productivity, inadequate irrigation, and inefficient supply chains. The manufacturing sector faces challenges such as low capacity utilization, outdated technology, and inadequate investment in research and development. The services sector, which accounts for the largest share of GDP, suffers from low productivity, a lack of skilled labor, and inadequate regulation. The trade and investment sector suffer from insufficient foreign direct investment, poor export competitiveness, and weak economic policies.

To address these challenges, Pakistan needs sustained investment in infrastructure, energy, education, and health. There is also a need to promote good governance, transparency, and accountability, and combat corruption. The development of renewable energy can help reduce Pakistan's reliance on imported oil, and the promotion of energy efficiency can reduce energy demand and promote sustainable development.

Overall, the current economic crisis in Pakistan is a multifaceted challenge that requires a comprehensive and sustained approach to address the root causes and promote sustainable development.

B. Recommendations

Based on the issues highlighted in the previous sections, the following are some recommendations for addressing the economic crisis in Pakistan:

1. Promote Investment: The government needs to improve the investment climate by promoting a stable and predictable policy environment. This can be achieved through measures such as simplifying regulations, reducing bureaucratic hurdles, and improving the judicial system to ensure contract enforcement.

2. Focus on Infrastructure Development: The government needs to prioritize investment in infrastructure, including transport, energy, and water supply. This will help improve the productivity of the economy and attract private investment.

3. Develop Human Capital: Investment in education and health is critical to develop human capital and improve productivity. The government needs to increase spending on education and health, improve access to these services, and promote public-private partnerships to improve the quality of education and healthcare.

4. Improve Governance: The government needs to improve governance by promoting transparency and accountability, strengthening the rule of law, and combating corruption. This will help create a level playing field for businesses, reduce transaction costs, and attract investment.

5. Promote Export Competitiveness: The government needs to promote export competitiveness by improving the business environment, investing in research and development, and reducing trade barriers. This will help increase exports and improve the balance of payments.

6. Improve Agriculture Productivity: The government needs to invest in irrigation infrastructure, improve access to credit and technology, and promote research and development to improve agriculture productivity.

7. Promote Renewable Energy: The government needs to promote renewable energy sources such as solar, wind, and hydropower to reduce the reliance on imported oil and promote sustainable development.

8. Address Energy Crisis: The government needs to address the energy crisis by investing in energy infrastructure, promoting energy efficiency, and diversifying the energy mix to reduce dependence on imported oil.

9. Address Fiscal Deficit: The government needs to address the fiscal deficit by reducing non-development expenditures, improving tax collection, and increasing exports to improve revenue.

10. Promote Public-Private Partnerships: The government needs to promote public-private partnerships to leverage private sector investment and expertise in infrastructure development, education, and healthcare.

These recommendations require a sustained and comprehensive approach by the government and other stakeholders to address the root causes of the economic crisis in Pakistan and promote sustainable development.

C. Final Thoughts

The economic crisis in Pakistan is a complex and multifaceted problem that requires a comprehensive and sustained approach to address the underlying causes. The issues highlighted in this book include low economic growth, high inflation, fiscal deficits, low foreign exchange reserves, poor governance, corruption, and weak infrastructure. These issues are interlinked and require a coordinated effort by the government, private sector, and civil society to address them.

Pakistan has immense potential for economic growth and development, given its strategic location, natural resources, and young and growing population. However, realizing this potential requires a commitment to reforms and investments in critical areas such as education, health, infrastructure, and governance. The recommendations provided in this book provide a roadmap for addressing the economic crisis in Pakistan and promoting sustainable development. It is now up to the government and other stakeholders to take action and implement these recommendations to improve the economic outlook of the country and the well-being of its people.

****